Hiding to Nothing

Hiding to Nothing

Anita Pati

First published 2022 by
Liverpool University Press
4 Cambridge Street
Liverpool
L69 7ZU

British Library Cataloguing-in-Publication data
A British Library CIP record is available

ISBN 978-1-800-85482-6 softback

Typeset by Carnegie Book Production, Lancaster
Printed and bound in Poland by Booksfactory.co.uk

For Ishaan

Train Triolet
(16.46 to Brighton)

I won't blow you up because I'm brown,
O twitchy woman who grassed up my shopping.
I went to the loo not to twiddle my belt.
I won't blow you up because I'm brown.
Terrorists don't tend to buy Cath Kidston
unless I am a cleanskin moron.
Because I'm brown, I won't blow you up,
O *native* woman who grassed up my shopping.

Olive Ridley

The world is my turtle, or I am.
Do I slip out from coral to crush it,
both skulls recoiling?

Or swoop to reef and mother-of-pearl
as the world hangs in nothing?

Will I tangle in trawlers, smother
in anchors, seaweed?

Perhaps I'll crack, let them harvest
my nested eggs
                          and display me –

Or make me to soup,
flick ash in my back, or might I

cradle in shell, so green
I can't see the world?

Or shall I wait until ripened,
swim free, to find
the world is now coral, or I am?

"she's in stocks, and shares"

gently we pored her   blading
from gilded throat down erector
spinae to gut marvel.

when she was filleted
and each piece packaged in dainty foils
bowed with taffeta, we settled her

in the river to float
upstream along wildebeest and bison rot,
which she upended, and swelled

from 'til all her pieces:
buttock, knee pad, the garnet ovum
like a spinning Mars, returned us

such bounty   we

we
tried to gum her back,
a little wonky

seams suppurating
a little pus and bounced
her sweet frame

in our hybrid SUVs,
our honeyed driveways,
our loft conversions.

but when she shrivelled, we sold her and that was that.

The Good Doctor,

like the dog that sniffs
out cancer,
            or truffles,
scents the girl
who thinks she's ugly,
fondles her in full view
because she is nobody
better, and nobody suspects
the good doctor
in his consulting room
of Parma Violets. And also,
she's vapour.

But so *there*:
bracefaced, yellowing
already, best candidate
for a life of stains:
tobacco, semen,
a slipstream of cock-ups.
So who else
would he doctor
before retiring
to Goofy Golf in Florida?

He examines breasts
stifled in a boy vest, gasps
at the hornetty acne
that masks her velvet pelt.

The God Doctor,
with his committees
and breath
like a scraped cheek
specimen, nooses her
blood pressure belt
bends her over –
that shivering girl –
because her hormones
are squiffy and perhaps

.

      Anyway,
he reasons, he was not her first
(to make her all empty)
so let her be her own last.

Cycular

When the floods spate again through the flat's front door
and the toddler coughs, outside's snuck in, sodden walls seeded,
                    plaster blisters like cigarette burns
on forgotten

These are the rivers of the north: swollen Irwell
Calder, Ouse, breaching an eschar where the gold fat glistens
                    and the white blood foams
in our plastic buckets.

And the reek of a childhood seeps through these walls:
rotgulley whip overflow
                    fantail of milfoil, valleymist rainfall,
triggering sirens.

When the oozages foam in their ministrations
but nobody listens – when they do, you're a cipher or a pain
                    or a duty but not love; where do you go
now for succour or for someone

to stop it? How to be counted when your voice is the bubble
that your small child blows, when the sky's drowning lungs
                    burst into downpour?
When it's soaked into earth,

only earth can listen, mainlining water in some stinking glory,
sending it pulsing into sewage-piped lowrise
                    because who cares for us?
You go on, you go on.

(like my infant soles)

Self-Portrait Exaggerating My Unknown Features

(after Adrian Piper's Self-Portrait Exaggerating My Negroid Features, *1981)*

Romping from the Sundarbans to Wimbledon,
roaming eye patched under pelt, plum lip, blood iris,
my hennaed hands bare Shellac™ nails, trained to scratch
your judging mouth. My unmapped features will not shut up.
So flatten my ribs – coral under your divers' feet –
here's my East End Ghee belly fleeing controlling pants.
Enough of my nose (it knows) and man will it scent you out,
sliced onto the Scoville scale of vehemence.
Yet times my war calls vapourise once hitting air;
I sweat behind skin-lightening Hollywood mango cream.
And when black curls sprout from your wooden, straight, blonde floors,
you'll swipe the roots to find peroxide gritting there.
And so you know my made-up face? I make me up.
I'll echo me, I'll echo us, we won't shut up.

Dodo Provocateur

Europeans hunted you mercilessly,
because you beakies wouldn't be doves or albatross.
Those whitish irises probably grotted and balled and seized,
black undertail coverts jutting at strumpet-starved sailors,
marooned on Mauritius, exotic, just not Bideford, Perth or Poole.
Why gobble pebbles big as nutmegs to temper your guts,
and prove fresh meat for rusky sailors, declaring you foul?
'Belly and breast pleasant enough in flavour,' they said.
If only they'd waited a few decades later before they snuffed you
forever, for being cloven-footed, turkey! You know,
you and your bulging brethren could have been common as peacocks,
not stuffed through your hooks in old Copenhagen or folded in sketchbooks.
Mauritian Martha, who froze your fruity body in gin?
Now of the Marthas exists only bitty skin, you pigeons.

Ruched Sock Rebels

Shrimport rarely shines; like northern towns
all up the coast, its punk is trammelled under rocks.
Mondays, post-my-therapy, we'd gabber, us
Lady Scruffs among the screwy perms and tans.
Legs in ruched knee socks, we giggled at your swanks
of minky cats, vowed not to work at Morrisons.
Your mum banned me, said I'd killed her baby;
dashed your head down from the clouds into the Irish Sea.

*I could never
mother another
like they mothered
me, never.*

Greenface

*The death of self-esteem can occur quickly, easily in children,
before their ego has "legs"[.]*
                    Toni Morrison, *The Bluest Eye*

The girl who cracked
            mirrors turned heads:
they fried hers
            with their mercurial backchat.
Times she was invisible and
            times the black ghost.

She shamed mirrors to face walls. Stole them back, pasting
their silver on vellum, daub, lassoing them in dreamcatchers.

Wore a kaleidoscope cloak of mirrored tiles and cracked
every one   she is thinking.

Since a tiny, plaited child, folk said she was /wyrd /

She lived among the dunes
            where girls with sandy hair
                        squatted natterjack toads
                                    astride her belly
                                                at duskfire parties.

This made her face divoted, turfy, diverted. Devoted.
Almost green.

Oooof, pooof,   *we'll blow your house down!*

is Girl playing
is she not
can we string her
to the drain
can we take her
home to show
our mum?
can we take a polaroid?

She knew she didn't have the bluest eye.

The white poplar trembles in the wind like an aspen — a willowy quiver of a girl.

Grandma's calendar with the three blonde sisters took pride of place in the Rajasthani village. *Will the grey skies make your eyes blue when you get there, didi?*

One day the townsfolk ate the white meat of her irises
with a dessert fork, Guernsey butter and garlic grubs.
Plus chips and curry sauce.

Luckily, she couldn't see this // sadly.
Because she was a witch, they grew back.

Stove my heart in.
It's piping hot one day
cowers like placebo the next:
stove it in.
I can build it up
to punnets of plums
pulsing juice but.
Crush it in a box.
Crust its outsides
with pink peppercorns,
griddle it with liver,
stove it.

Such good spoken English!

The Girl Who Would Be King

Is it English streets are paved with gold,
Papa? Where chaps sport bowler hats
to hide their rice for dinner?

Guess no one wears chappals but Tower Jewel heels
that soar to heaven, and their feet don't pickle?

Bet there's no hullabaloos over pilfered mooli
or rapscallion cockroaches to flaunt bottoms at me.
Plus no antsy pantsy.

May I squat in a red telephone box
and pray to Dr Who?

They're not all bloody bastards like you say,
Papa, you nincompoop!

Mr Kipling will give me a French Fancy
then croon:

Roxanne, you pretty princess.

But I will call myself Joanna
and eat jackfruit jelly with Eton litter.

Policemen will give me fishunchips
or clips on the ear.

This is the fair play in England, says Mr Mishra.

What the Dickens, Papa, will they think of me,
Graham Greene and HG Wells and
those noble and free

                            like the Queen?

When we go to live there and shoo their monkeys
off their ruddy faces, they might thank us?

Paperdolls

or

Where Are My Curly Scrolls of Sisters?

They are wedging me open with lapwings, the feathers
angled and birded to hurt. But I've a tight heart.

Dad took the call, uprooted the brood to bacon barmcakes.
Here we're tiny, a fistful of morula, massing.

A leper sold us salted cucumber in newspaper twists
then slipped drainwards *that's where you come from*

your hands are dirty, sssshhhh shut your mouth while you eat
said the mynah bird, no, said the settlers.

Mum escaped through airmail script to slinky heat.
That upfaced tooth extracts its roots; such a mossy cliff.

The cliff is crocheted pearl, gnatty whirlpools, round ligaments.
Where are my larvic, volcanic sisters?

I'd crouch in the boiler room, making ski lifts from off Blue Peter.
If we'd stayed I'd have been the biggest family,

you're so quiet we thought you'd disappeared: sssshhhh
cut me a row of paperdoll aunties –

keep cutting inside me with your instruments. You are making holes
for light to get in. I'll stay in Recovery if you nurse me.

Where are my mockingbirds for sisters?
Tetra Pak houses, rainy terraces, grey, no laughters.

I've threaded the mothers on daisy chains which I pluck
some times. Plant in oasis.

Turmeric lightens the skin: we've become cream boaters and lace.
Fold up your plaits, village girl. I know I lapse; please keep trying.

Others said: too nosey cheeky lippy heady hairy kneedy
hearty   too faceless chinless holey ...

EVERY BODY BIT WRONG

Some loved her, fudged and sinful.   Hibiscus in the gin.

                                !

She bumped into the air void where her self should be.
Drummed at its diaphragm   but couldn't get in.

Where are you?   Mirror, mirror on the wall.

And the men?

how many of us never call it?

because when you smash your head
like a pumpkin on the *Incarnadine* door frame,
having siphoned the party's Malbec
at a townhouse in Stoke Newington,

ethanol spearing darts through the gloom,
everyone too sober, in control, for you,
teen years caught up
like flames at your skirts,

polite chat, minted verbena, NO
and he pickets your elbow, and people's laughs –
see the couple fly so witty that Man that professional
Man with the footballer curls, that Man's
sluicy arm that projects you too hard,

that Man who *protects*: it's your own stupid fault.
i've never called it, but
reformed friends need you to leave,
ciao go away good to see you next time.

still today you think it was you
after wine, doesn't matter
what happened, it was me.

and all you knew was the charity worker, dapper, yes,
his ex-wife an author but him, met him twice,

at your back, Victorian squat with Last FM streaming
and only your screams like nothing you know
escaped your mouth since

shouldn't have drunk, was me
couldn't stop, rolled in carpet like that

such an intricate ceiling rose, these townhouses, one day i'll live
in one, still i've said nothing and who knows

least me, drink and me close up your wineshame, that mouth
that wine shut your mouth

Manju

Because he liked the toddy,
because he twinkled for her,
he beat her.
Because he towered and
she was a bird,
because he was soused
and the kerosene cask
to cook sabzi
exploded it seems and.
Because her nylon saree
of plum and curd
kindled and flared,
the thatch flamed
like spathodea
and the roof withered —
he creased back her throat
to see the sky.
Because she laboured
with filigree wrists of bone,
a waist you could twist,
to feed her boys, because
because the littler pined to be
an American *rocket* star,
his head bent up —
the rain came in and
she'd take his whipping
always again
on her keloid skin
because through the gap
in the broken hut
she saw only stars.

Domestic

It was only the oven you couldn't fathom,
the angled tray not fitting its grooves
that night in June when the burnt tower happened
hotwhite in our highrise, so scared.
We are bending not to be broken.
And you bellowed and raged like a man inside out,
every hurt from childhood washed onto me, why
O God not the neighbours, knocking our door up.
The children definitely slept through it all.

The police are here. *Don't be offended I'm sorry*
I have to ask you these. He's not violent – a doctor!
Has he ever tried to isolate you
from your family, has he ever withheld money
followed you, strangled or hurt your children?
The children definitely slept through it all.
Or threatened you, ever shouted so loud
that the neighbours thought I am a bartered soul
He's decent. He is. *Are you frightened of him?*

Are you frightened of him? He's decent. He is.
Have the neighbours thought I am a bartered soul
or shouted so loud, or ever threatened?
The children definitely slept through it all.
Ever followed, strangled or hurt your children?
Has he ever withheld money, your family
has he ever tried to isolate you?
I have to ask you these. He's not violent, a doctor!
The police are here. *Don't be offended I'm sorry.*

The children definitely slept through it all.
O God not the neighbours, knocking our door up
every hurt from childhood washed onto me, why?

And you bellowed and raged like a man inside out.
We are bending not to be broken.
So scared, hotwhite in our highrise,
that night in June when the burnt tower happened,
the angled tray not fitting its grooves.
It was only the oven you couldn't fathom.

/wyrd /

Some days her body splayed forest, brain gnarled and open like a pine cone.
Bugs would slide into ridges. Other days resin breezed between ribs.
Sundays let the stream in to watch tiddlers leap from her eye sockets.
Her words skittered themselves into a hive from where she peered.
Her womb was wide as a gurnard and twice as scarlet.
Her heart was full with griddled liver.
Lodged in the mirror fissure. No celebration between worlds.
No festival, no ritual, just a streak of silver.

23

NoMo

I won't make
that I'm a puss or a fish (or a bird)
to write about this; just that
daily I claw my own roster,
beak through my womb
because I couldn't swim, slink or fly.

*

pop pop too many children already in the world pop so why don't
you pop an orphan in your pocket pop

*

– How old are yours?

_   "   "

_   "   "

*

don't
invite
her
to the
baby
shower
she'll
booze
and
blubber

awkward!
hissy missy
mad
cat lady
too much
you know
what
she's
like
(left it too late)

                              Sofia
                    *
                              Ozzy
              *
                                Jayden
        *
                                  Mia
      *
                                    Noah
    *
                                      Ellora
      *
                                    Jackson
        *
                                  Sonny
          *
                                Karnatika
            *
                              Harry
              Pearl   Amrita

*

I don't want to do this to myself.
And upstairs the woman with four kids
knocks out another.
And downstairs that dad swears at his toddler.
And I inject ovary from Chinese hamster.
Though I have eggs I have eggs I have eggs.
Each time they ask, "how old are yours?"
I'm gaily like it doesn't matter.
This, for the rest of my life?
Tell me what to do.

*

All eyes cast downward in our own private hells beneath trefoil insignia Heart FM blasts out mortgages and 90s' teeny bop How did we end up seated around a rug branded LIFE with its fake white orchids? Have they grown? Did we make a follicle popsicle? Will we win this scan? Whirr that credit card machine *yes we can* Another 40-minute wait while we winch out regrettables Meantime machines gurgle chocolate cappuccinos wailing of well-stocked coffee within a red-walled pouch pulsing empty Our little butterbean

*

they have harvested eggs
tiny spherical miracles
that never smell the air
tonight with whispers
they will murmur to each other
on stacks of shelves
in humming incubators
we leave them to tether

*

Stay with us, please.

Sometimes a hornet
          burrows into my vein
bats through me like a pinball
          to burst fizzy
from my mouth
          and slap your sparky skin
so both of us brink
          at the edge of friendship
where we sail parallel
          your family life
my quiet one
          why don't you understand?

                              *

Stay wit

                              *

          CAN'T YOU JUST REAR HORSES?

                              *

You're such a violent little pony, under the knife again.
cloddites   from your rabid   frilly
                                 must we sink you with your   bruised pubic smile?
Spilt froth,   Convulse that mane,   next time maybe.
incisions!

When you retch, you hurl
                    mouth.

What black gut liquor!
Incisions

*

NOT   THIS   TIME

*

How you caused havoc
little trailblazer.
O you got yourself into a pickle.

Finally, I was alive,
mother, nose tingling
with petrol and cinnamon.

You stretched me.
This belly fed on wine
bowed to you.

How you tickled –
fired me to bed or
poppy seed cake.

And for a few weeks
we three were family
for the first time.

So thank you, shy robin
teetering on turned soil;
you showed us fleet joy.

*

Baby loss weasels itself beneath the torso, bilge in the milk. A white dad stares at me in East India Dock, grabs his daughter's hand. Kid girl with the emerald eyes. I'll eat your child. Thumbwail of baby smeared in my mind's eye, steeped in embryonic brine.

So I howled like a dog in a hinge. You know how some days you smack through, pane after pane? Well, he positioned the camera and my bloods fell like dead eggs.

Pummelheads fist like strung pork knuckle, decorating my insides for Christmas. A flute of bile tipped down my throat. *Oh kids are such HARD WORK / YOU can traipse the world!* Those people say we're winners.

*

I reek of non-motherhood while they have life ladled into their mouths.

*

Waking daily with a hammer
claw pincering inside and the cries
of my kith and my kin blown wide

*

Sour woman let her milk curdle. (... she left it too late ...)

*

There is a silence in the non-mum where we swallowed our little one; you can always tell us.
We carry ours around like you do in your sling. Curly air sac in the lungs, an extra breath where we forgot
to laugh, the top note of a screech that's not ours. And we keep it tight in an umbilical stranglehold.

*

My mind/
    has squawked/
        and flown/today/
            while I/
                face down/
                    and let/
                  the flock/
             mow me/
         slowly/under
      ground/
    until they/
turn/
    their tails/
        and feather air/
            into my lungs/

*

Too Much Birdsong

Fine, she can crane over the tea estates. But those fertile
Munnar hillslopes fuzz too much her thighs. Monsoon
is a *digestif* swiped down the throat, teasing
creepers into secret niches.

Hornbills must be coming!

Too many tourists at this time of year
with their drowned mobiles and syncopated hearts.
She'll loosen their betelnut boxes: *woad* for English patients,
chandan for wealthy Indians weekending from Mumbai.

Mischief, this female.

Bluesy Nilgiri flycatchers make her internals tic.

Those scarlet minivets flaming at windows, startling babies.
Tis pity 'tis a chore to feel this every day: to see centipedes pink
as her palm brush into foetal curls then roll down clay roof tiles.

The mists blow through her belly.

There's an eco-lodge where kids at breakfast spin appam
on their fingers. Troubadours! Mothers
stroke shoulders. Crickets tickle at green language
and chirr like squeaked knees.

The elephant bells have bust open their violet petals
after rain rinse. Eucalyptus shudder; life splits out.

Perhaps she's a goddess – this big, this tall, haunches to lie
for. But she can't stop the birdsong baffling from her womb.
How to stop the birdsong?

Cuckoo

I'll have a scar that smiles at nothing
where no baby hung.

Now surgeons dip for rugby balls of muscle
under yolky fat, eggs blown and carapaced
to knock my heart out.

It's a trick of endometrium embroidery;
machinists in a race to score red pinpricks
just before the anaesthesia lifts.

I'm raw to their advances in the theatre lights:

Here's our moment!

So the winner swoops, lifts out the glistening heads

– first wail in air –

then plopped into the kidney bowl, they slither,
fibroid, breathless in the world and now unbirthed,
metabolise; pedunculated stalks, those eyes,

a blinkered peek   *are we your joy?*

Worthless, they're discarded. Thieving
freeloaders that gorged on my blood riches.

And which doctor notched his post
with fine-stitched purses?
Plaudits for the neatest wombs?
Has he children in his home?

In time I'm prodded out until forlorn
and failed my sutures clench into this cheat's embrace.

In final, cut and proven, everywoman.

Bloodfruit

Naked in the mirror, I look at my face, my boobs, belly, those legs, side-eye my bum, poke out my tummy, everything's there, so why can't I, why not build baby?

I'm unprecious cargo: not a real woman. My body's betrayed me.

Q. Are we only worthy when we've procreated?
A. YES?

Q. But what is a woman anyway?   A. Had enough of you woke-folk, I can just tell you how I feel.

<u>mantras</u>

I don't deserve to be happy; I don't deserve a family; I don't deserve this life.

Too fat to be a mum.
Too poor to be a mum.
Too ugly to be a mum.
Too old to be a mum.
Too fucked to be a mum.

ZOOM ZOOM ZOOM, WE'RE GOING TO THE MOON!

What bit of me is broken? It's a white emptiness in my head like I surrender **all the colour in the world went** infertility washes me gone, shattered rock at Kilve beach – my flag is up – trample me off the pavement you mums with kiddies: my body is not my own. I'm done.

     –   *I had anorexia as a teenager so always knew my fertility could be tricky.*

Obese they keep telling me but I pump iron like the best
of them. The NHS makes me feel like some fat, disgusting
whale that doesn't deserve to have kids. I'm 26.

I was chubby, fat cow! they said. Took me 'til 38 before I let
go of the body hang-ups. Worried about looking fat
if pregnant, having to go up clothes sizes.

I look back at pictures of me at 29 and think why
did you give yourself such a headache?
Yeah, body image has affected mine and X's sex,
trying to conceive.

Q. Isn't this all a bit vain?

A. If I eat food, I'm scared they'll bully me fatty like they
did at puberty, call me dirty. So I try not to eat in front of
anybody.

Q. What's this got to do with you not having a child?

before i met my husband, i went through a rape
and i kept feeling that
maybe because i let it happen it was my Fault
and that was the reason behind the infertility
and even though i'm not religious like God was trying
to say to me it's your Fault it happened
so I'm taking your fertility away from you and
it took a lot
of reality checks to realise that's not the case,
if God is there
he wouldn't do that
to someone and it's never your Fault
if you're the victim, it's the person
who did it that's
at Fault

Q. AND YOU! WHY DID YOU LEAVE IT TOO LATE, CAREER WOMAN?

Perhaps you've met women like me? Flinty, driven, abortions akimbo? Judge me like all the others do. I'm 58, too old now – a step-mum, half a mum, not allowed to wholeheart mum.

Careered ahead instead of kids, fecund teen me, lush as placenta peat though maybe I was emotionally barren, go on say BARREN relationships festered. How could I ask for kiddies after that first dear baba? You see my ex stalked and raped me, then I had to deliver my dead baby on my 19th birthday and how could I ever have gone there again

but I've had a good life, I've had to O God and now I care for my mother, tell me who will be there for me?

But stop! if you soften — I warn you I'm tough: when my stepson announced his adoption, my torso enstuffed like a tailor's dummy, yes I'd be grandma but never a mum, **it doesn't end**, grief, it sidles, surges, slackens then throttles your mettle, jealousy, shame, and you'd be there too if you had been me, not lucky enough to mother — but we're banned from admitting the anger because who are we? Childless women: base in the pecking order.

Some nights, my arm aches in its marrow, the right,
where I'd have cradled a babe, and I sob
like the mamas and babas do but still how do you
judge me?

hush little baby, don't say a word

Good *Grief* woman! Take the Clomid
and be done with it!

So we did IVF. (Or **I**t's **V**ery **F**rankenstein as my friend once said.)

As a vicar I stand at the altar with wine and bread, sermon on life and death, Jesus, take services for mothers. Most have no idea about my own body, my bloods... I run funerals for others; now grief has hit me like a truck. And my husband doesn't care if we have children or not.

I'm childless but God is bigger, hope is bigger   x x

I was pregnant for a tiny time
we made babies – that bond –
the day the embryos went in
the freezer was the day I became
Mother.

(Although it's hard to be a Christian with spare embryos.)

I was miscarrying perfect embryos and they couldn't stop it
I was miscarrying perfect embryos and they couldn't stop it
I was miscarrying perfect embryos and they couldn't stop it
I was miscarrying perfect embryos and they couldn't stop it
I was miscarrying perfect embryos and they couldn't stop
and everyone thinks IVF is a miracle, it's

life that is a miracle. God is bigger than this; hope is bigger than this. It's when I go to bed that it's visceral; I can only sleep cuddling a pillow because the emptiness in my womb, my breasts, is so feverish.

      Am I allowed to speak my grief? To stand up in church and say I grieve, like you for your absent and dead, I too grieve for my neverborn? Will you tire and tell me to get over it? One day at the altar I'll tell you because so many of us are silent.

SHUSH ON THE FAILING, SHUSH NOW

The mothers are complaining while nothing in my body works.

The cysts springcoil like adders while the mothers are so stressed.

You're so lucky, look! they say. You're drinking rum! Yes.

THE CRYOPRESERVATION BAR COCKTAIL LIST

CHOOSE BEFORE THEY THAW:
EMBRYOS ON ICE, IN STRAWS

millions frozen globally in subterranean laboratories
agony of indecision; keening IVF babies

SLIPPERY NIPPLE
Clarified milk, we pray for this, Sambuca, Champagne.
Avoid ice.

STRAWBERRY DAIQUIRI
Ripe blastocyst berries steeped in white rum, lucky
to have *frosties,* lime, maraschino syrup. Ice.

MOCKTAIL
Peach tea cordial. Cleavage-stage embryos living in liquid
nitrogen with Ayurvedic bitters. Iced.

NEGRONI – stirred, not shaken
Sloe gin, secondary infertility in purple, Noilly Prat (sweet
vermouth), do we stop our family at 2/3/4? Campari. Ice.

GIMLET
Botanical gin, painful, screwy handtool aka embryo
storage insurance policy, lime 'cordial' and 'zest'. Ice.

PROCRASTINATION TWISTER
Grey Goose, Mia's sister's in the freezer: implant, thaw
(perish), donate (experiments, the desperate). Fucking ice.

LIMBO LEMON CHASER
Coconut syrup. Can't kill 'em, can't use 'em, eternal death-
in-life, peated Irish whiskey, lemon peel. Ice.

OBLIVION WITH AN UMBRELLA
Absinthe, dose of erasure, Angostura and coffee bitters,
soda. Ice.

**Yellow bird, up high on banana tree, yellow bird,
you sit all alone like me.**

#*I could never mother another like they mothered*

Give me
the mothers'
exhaustion,
their thwarted
ambitions,
their tedium,
give me even
their psychoses —
I would give
anything
to not have this.

Get over it!

Lactic

I found myself running, running out the bad blood
like a bat slicing through my head I wasn't here but
sluicing out wormwoods at the Anglo-Saxon churchyard,
flown through haylofts, nighting out my fret,
pounding my feet, three miscarriages behind me,
each little heart stopped, each at 7 weeks,
was when my own heart stopped, sailing the drifts,
wings like a purled shawl battening down upwinds.
I carry these babies everywhere I go, over water meadows,
municipal clockbacks, others ignore them, spiked
onto pinions – my starry hearts – or now warmed cellular
and lodged into muscle meat, tingling at my calves,
and though I have a daughter now, and could move forward,
they settle in flesh memory, running through the blood.

One of you, two, buckle your shoe
then scram! **You're no family!**
Three, four: unbolted door 😊

I'd always dreamed Dad
would take my kids back
to Dominica where he grew up –
show them swamp bloodwoods
but it's here it all ends: I'm
the last flameburst fruit
on this vine Daddy holds.

Try, try harder, adopt?
IVF, just don't give up!
You'll win but don't be shhhhh!
the haggy, childless woman!

39 years 'til I'd find him
who'd raise a family with me.
But no pulse thrums in his heart's
sac now for either of us.
And this is never the fairy tale
that they sold me. Though I strike on,
old women insist they pray for me.

– they always say your time will come but you have to be realistic because maybe it won't.

– in your thirties, there is still that hot shimmer of possibility. Which makes being childless allowable, forgivable. You hit your forties, fertility vanishes, you're menopausal, irrelevant. You vanish.

– infertility is lonely even with a loving husband.

– When your childhood's messed up, you delay adolescence and before you know it, it's too late.

– it's a different form of grief; more intense than losing my dad.

#some days I just surrender to the pit; insanity or marathons aren't me.

– I've had mentally abusive relationships, and this, but you wake up the next day and carry on. I went and got my nails done with the girls.

– there's no respite for us. You come back through your front door and you're back in these four walls
where everything happens: the peeing on the stick,
the taking the supplements, the little babygro you've got
hung up in your bedroom with Some Miracles Take Longer
Than Others spread on its front.

#not this time!

I could never mother another like she mothered me, never.
That's why some of us don't mother. How could I open
my breast sacs if they'd chafen a tiny throat? You think I'm 50,
career cheerleader, never been fafa for babies,
ghosted in my corner, ashen and puce: what do you know?

Rural Ireland was safe then but winters a pitiless snow-wall.
I remember tarred fences ice-strung with creosote baubles.
We skated lakes in red wellies   mother was no protector.
They squalled like love was toxic; I didn't stand a chance.
I didn't stand a chance. Some call it ambivalence.

My parents swallowed my childhood. This is not how you're mummy.
Men wanted my babies; I hurt them like *they* had hurt me.
My mind said no kids but my body said yes: I was blooming.
Then my mind said yes but my body could not. So when mother died,
I slipped into icy water, mouth bubbling to be fed.

No one taught fertility then so don't be a motherhood flasher.
How do you know that riddle you're quizzing hasn't just had
       womb cancer?
You're only a person of value, it seems, if you can be a mother.
I thought I was damaged because they were damaged, and so the
       cycle goes.
And now I'm finally 50, Lord help me, still I don't know.

"My brother has nightmares about his own children dying,
and I say you can imagine
what it's like, it's a fucking nightmare and like, who wants to
go there in their imagination? It's a terrifying place to go,
I've sensed the fear in people who have kids. I imagine
had my little ones lived I'd have lived in daily fear of a bad
thing happening to them."

I will abridge my story for you:

My boys died on the day they were born and they are my sons.
It's lonely being a mum without kids I can show to the world.
I'm proud of them like any other mother but
telling mums this makes them fear and once, they'd tell me adopt
but now I'm older, folks are stumped what to say –
so we'll tell you our tale. (But quickly for I sense your horror.)

ASK ME THEIR NAMES

They come to me along the bay. That's where we walk,
me, daddy and the dogs beside the slopes of downy birch.
Sometimes, the boys, they're centrifugal, parting the sky
over the Arran mountains just as the sun pierces.
Or they sparkle in the frost on a cockleshell. Or they're
in the eyes of a hare that has spotted us, in that split second
of assessment before it takes off.

We tried so hard for years and then they came
and left at 20 weeks my boys my boys.
This term is when they'd start their school at five,
this Christmas when they'd decimate their toys.
Some days I just surrender to the pit;
insanity or marathons aren't me.
Who celebrates the mother never lived?
Or children gone without a chance to be?
But really nice to meet them and I know:
The grainy scan showed Pete in disco dance.
And Herbie, sulky, sucked his thumb at birth.
And though I only met my twin boys once,
they'll visit daily into my old age;
we'll playdate every day. And yes, I rage.

"I've not lost them like keys, some careless mishap; my boys
are here."

Guess what? I loved being pregnant!
It had taken so long and I'd chat to the mums
on cramping and sherbet lime jellies.
And then there's that moment –
I'm scratched from the group.
Ghost-mum against the allies.

HOW DO I MOTHER THESE CHILDREN NO LONGER RUNNING ABOUT ON THIS EARTH? IT'S SO LONELY THESE WILDS, MY BLOSSOMS BERTH IN WHITE. THEY'RE – HERBIE, YOU TINKER – THEY'RE – PETE, YOU FOTHERGILL, FOAMING THIS SEA, YOU CHEEKY FOSSERGILL, BIG HANDS LIKE YOUR DADDY'S, READY TO WORK ON A BUILDING SITE, SPADES FOR FINGERS, HAMHOCKS FOR THIGHS. AND HERBIE, HEART FACE AND ROSEBUD MOUTH, PLAY YOUR PIANO WITH THOSE FLOWERY FINGERS, SLIDING YOUR LIMBS LIKE RAZORSHELL CLAMS. SUCH DIFFERENT BROTHERS. PETE, WOULD YOU STOP THE BULLIES OFF HERBIE? HERB, WILL YOU PAINT YOUR MUMMY OUR MOUNTAIN BEHIND WHERE WE LIVE, YOU ME DOGS AND DADDY? WILL YOU LOOK AFTER US, BOYS, WHEN WE AGE, WILL YOU DRIVE US DOWN LANES, YOUR AULD YINS?

THERE IS A POEM, IT'S FAMOUS, DO YOU KNOW IT?

i carry your heart with me(i carry it in
my heart)

e my words but
s too much, I can't
ead it when it's published.

When we were little, we would giggle,
wouldn't we? At my wooden doll's house
with Crittall windows that Dad
put real lights into, and you'd dress
the boy in tights and what did we know
then at 7? I thought we'd both have families.

But you ... and me ... you never
know how it will turn out.
I'm on this earth

~~only once and it didn't happen.~~
~~I know it was hard for you too.~~

#then he gifted me his birth and

THE NEONATAL WARD

–   When the staff call you *all* Mummy,
    is it in case we babies flatline,
    or because they don't know
    your name, Mummy? Time
    for my cares, Mummy! Dip the NG
    tube in my belly acid, thrust it up
    my nose when I pull it out, because
    prems don't feel pain, Mummy!

–   My teenagers cook meat stew for me
    when I get back from the ward
    evenings. They ask about their baby
    sister alone every night at the end
    of the tube line.

–   Hey astronauts floating in your shared
    amniotic sac, bleached faces downcast.

–   The postnatal ward was worst. I could
    hear all these other mums joyous,
    breasting their newborns and my babies
    were downstairs in ICU plugged
    to machines being fed from catheters.

–   I pray then make chicken curry before
    the three oldest ones' school,
    their daddy's a taxi driver, he brings
    me here to the hospital where I pray
    for this boy, I pray at his bedside, I
    pray loud all day on my beads.

- For all the medical complications, my twin girls survived – how could I ever complain? They are a miracle.

- So tired I'd asked you to come early and suddenly you were here at 31 weeks. You were public property **for 2 months**, lived in a see-through box **for 2 months**, didn't breathe outside air **for 2 months**, Mummy could hardly hold you **for 2 months,** but you charmed the world.

- I'm the most grateful Mummy alive because mine made it
  #but I will never forget.

- Outside though! When you're a white woman with a brown baby, you're a slag; when you're a brown woman with a pale baby, you're the nanny.

- The staff on this ward are angels.

Mr Octopus for Preemies

From the black sky of our incubator – HELP US – you are the pole star Mother
saw and hurled herself towards through groggy egg sucks and headFks.
So I twist my woollen legs around the mermaid's wine glass and O don't you
have creamy dead man's fingers? Your sats monitor waves like kelp, bleep of quiet anemone.
Those agency nurses strap me to the corner while they drain aspirate from your milky belly; I
aspire to your love. But I've too much silt for milk. I'm waiting for the probes to satellite me
answers; they're such sly weed in the ocean box. Keep secret our white noise tank. Look
at Mother's fingers scrabbling through the port holes for you! Kelp startled by your heart,
kelp startled by your lungs, fronds making scribbles across that screen. I'm the octopus, Baba.
Old ladies with gnarled hands knitted me for you, snapping sticks for your balletic fingers.
Behold my plaited acrylic yarn, ye Mighty, and preen. You and me, don't let Mama in, we
can swim here.

Knitted toy octopi are used in incubators so babies can grab their legs rather than the wires.

HOW TO FEED A PREMATURE BABY (and other ephemera)

Plunge the nasogastric (NG) tube past his throat, oesophagus and into his gut. Several times a day if he has the audacity to rip it out. Help pin him down, sometimes with two nurses, so they can slink the snake down again for him to look at you, despite being minus nine weeks, like the traitor you feel.

Before each feed (8–12 times daily), drag back the pipette to dredge up residual milk in his gut. Drip it onto a strip of litmus paper in sunset amber, egg yolk, urine yellow or lime. You want the acid count, about 4.5. This means the NG tube is safely in his tummy. Repeat several times if you wrongly draw alkaline. When happy he is acid, dandle the syringe high and pour UHT longlife milk down the tube sometimes for 40 minutes. Breast milk if you're lucky this early. He may pull the tube out during.

In the 1.5 hours inbetween, eat, toilet, drink, rest, research your premature baby, get down to John Lewis to buy him babygros, breast pumps, bottles EXPRESS EXPRESS EXPRESS at a mint-green hospital grade pump. Fight for the pump machine, search other wards to find one. Fight for a screen. Find a nurse to give you plastic pumps. Wonder why so many are women of colour here. No one to wonder with. Finally travel home at 10pm, clean flat, cook, wash sterilise bottles, do laundry, research your premature baby, sleep, wake during sleep for that 3am creamy EXPRESS, up early again. Suppress all emotion or this will never get done. Reach out at 4am to the silent cot, remember he's in the plastic hospital box. Repeat until you hope to take him home maybe nine weeks/ four months/246 days later.

Before each feed (8–12 times daily), drag back the pipette to dredge up residual milk in his gut. Drip it onto a strip of litmus paper in sunset amber, egg yolk, urine yellow or lime. You want the acid count, about 4.5. This means the NG tube is safely in his tummy. Repeat several times if you wrongly draw alkaline. When happy he is acid, dandle the syringe high and pour UHT longlife milk down the tube sometimes for 40 minutes. Breast milk if you're lucky this early. He may pull the tube out during.

BEFORE EACH FEED (8—12 TIMES DAILY), DRAG BACK THE PIPETTE TO DREDGE UP RESIDUAL MILK IN HIS GUT. DRIP IT ONTO A STRIP OF LITMUS PAPER IN SUNSET AMBER, EGG YOLK, URINE YELLOW OR LIME. YOU WANT THE ACID COUNT, ABOUT 4.5. THIS MEANS THE NG TUBE IS SAFELY IN HIS TUMMY. REPEAT SEVERAL TIMES IF YOU WRONGLY DRAW ALKALINE. WHEN HAPPY HE IS ACID, DANDLE THE SYRINGE HIGH AND POUR UHT LONG-LIFE MILK DOWN THE TUBE SOMETIMES FOR 40 MINUTES. BREAST MILK IF YOU'RE LUCKY THIS EARLY. HE MAY PULL THE TUBE OUT DURING.

In the 1.5 hours inbetween, eat, toilet, drink, rest, research your premature baby, get down to John Lewis to buy him babygros, breast pumps, bottles EXPRESS EXPRESS EXPRESS at a mint-green hospital grade pump. Fight for the pump machine, search other wards to find one. Fight for a screen. Find a nurse to give you plastic pumps. Wonder why so many are women of colour here. No one to wonder with. Finally travel home at 10pm, clean flat, cook, wash sterilise bottles, do laundry, research your premature baby, sleep, wake during sleep for that 3am creamy EXPRESS, up early again. Suppress all emotion or this will never get done. Reach out at 4am to the silent cot, remember he's in the plastic hospital box. Repeat until you hope to take him home maybe nine weeks/ four months/246 days later.

Before each feed (8–12 times daily), drag back the pipette to dredge up residual milk in his gut. Drip it onto a strip of litmus paper in sunset amber, egg yolk, urine yellow or lime. You want the acid count, about 4.5. This means the NG tube is safely in his tummy. Repeat several times if you wrongly draw alkaline. When happy he is acid, dandle the syringe high and pour UHT longlife milk down the tube sometimes for 40 minutes. Breast milk if you're lucky this early. He may pull the tube out during.

Before each feed (8–12 times daily), drag back the pipette to dredge up residual milk in his gut. Drip it onto a strip of litmus paper in sunset amber, egg yolk, urine yellow or lime. You want the acid count, about 4.5. This means the NG tube is safely in his tummy. Repeat several times if you wrongly draw alkaline. When happy he is acid, dandle the syringe high and pour UHT longlife milk down the tube sometimes for 40 minutes. Breast milk if you're lucky this early. He may pull the tube out during.

Continue for weeks/months/until he can suck/is term, whichever comes sooner. Remember he's only alive because of this. Be grateful.

At the crest, cross-legged, they *ohhhmmm*.
Sun torches beams
through dawn vapour.
Sun wakens tinder –
Interrogator – bares naked
this week's searching, paying souls.

she bumped into the air void where her self

X

spells

on an unmade night
this heart kinks
      like an ace of spades in my skull
red Shiraz spooks up my veins

but
i come from nowhere quiet
soft sand
           she shut my heart and
though the blood beat
it never opened

still sky's grey drops
          into a pudsy gut
puddles wrinkle like twistwristskin

i blow into the seedy wind
          dodge crab apple floods
green gulls wheel harrumphs

rise out of bed
        sick to the core
        tick off minutes
watch them crash to the wall

and along the hurly knife blade sings
i'm open chest with foul blood steep
and sleep with its nimitars pools my dense
i'm awake but some times only

Her World Is Fury

Her as a pockled crab, hidden in shingle.
Her as spat-on sprat, slivered
bilged back in the Caspian sea.
Scuffed knees: Hers:
half-orange pitted skins:
calloused: Her bullet caps.

The slashed arms of Her: oil leaks
plunging through seawater.
Her voice, a whistle in the Wadi desert.
Her with the brown flower hands.
Her eyes a kingfisher's fanfare.
The belly of Her, sometimes crossfire.
Her eggs, drowsy bull eyes.

When Her puzzles, Her
wrinkles dance green
in the life monitor. And
Her hair trawls the nine worlds
birthed in a Nordic night. But the heart
of Her is bruise waiting bee-sting.
Her, whose soul tails lost swifts on the upwinds.
Her, whose wrath comes in thunder's four-second delay.

Routed

Is it you or you or you
who will bolt into my gaze,
my ear, my catastrophic

throat? Can you hear me
on the ninth floor peering at you
from my towerblock window here?

This gilded cube is where
my Marseillaise, my marching mind,
seeks minds of all calamities:

the wincing pulp, pupating
pipes in risers, aluminium denture
boxes; thrashing life is here –

cracks in my ear. I thought
of you; you rang. You heard
my song – my jana, gana, mana,

Ganga, knavish trickster pulse
I signalled out of concrete –
neurons sparking down

the network popping in my head
like mustard seeds in oil,
like faulty fuses, siren screams.

And you down there, bedevilled
and believed.

When I'm fossilised
in concrete, cradled through
the countless hours,

lusting after Georgian stucco,
quite *barbaric* tyranny,
you cut me off.

But still my chest frays open,
bivalved wires spitting, bloodish.
For your connects, I wait.

Cornershop Tulips

Like that, X was gone
in the way I thought might happen
to me, lots of us have thought
but it took X –
bawdy, boozy dog walker, to shame us
for not stopping her.

Wait 'til it's one of your own language
throwing themselves off the top floor.
You laughers, wait.

Silver Jubilee

She runs red crayon
around her bunched fingers
to draw knuckley flowers.

A bouquet of fists –
a family grabs hands –
limbs clashed in colours:

English maypole blues,
skin pinks,
a celebratory pageant on paper.

Her face, hushed,
is a copper ha'penny,
serene, like the Queen's,

when the brick gets in,
sailing like boats
she'd learned to fold as a toddler

to land square at her face
(kaleidoscoping
the patio glass)

from where their splinterous
GET BACK HOME! whoops
ransack the air. And no,

it's not fair that no-one will see
her picture now.
Should she draw it again?

—

When I was a golden Western
and my hair was victory,
I held no fear and
was weightless as wheat-ears.

The future did not loom beyond me
like night stars — a stagger
between points of light.

Tomorrow came straight,
hard as Blackpool rock,
pink like my infant soles.

Now I wake and hide my face:
lists smudge; my people are scant.
Bloods pillage my armour.
I wear a ragged eye-gag.

Days seem shapeshifters
kidding me through dustsheets.
The world is a vacant house
with no holiday.

Who will care for my little bobo
when our insides patchwork the sky
with crimson?

Notes and Acknowledgements

Thank you to the editors of the following publications where versions of some of these poems first appeared: *Aesthetica Creative Writing Award Anthology 2022*, *Butcher's Dog*, https://crossedlines.co.uk/routed/, *Finished Creatures*, *POEM*, *Poetry Birmingham*, *Poetry London*, *Poetry Review*, *The Rialto*, *Stand*, *The Times Literary Supplement*, *Under the Radar*.

A longer version of *Greenface* is published by Bad Betty Press (2019). Some poems appeared in my pamphlet, *Dodo Provocateur*, published by *The Rialto* (2019).

Bloodfruit: heartfelt thanks to Kate Brian, Holly Campbell-Carden, Marcella Carew, Jody Day, Lucy Dunbar, Emma FitzGerald, Jessica Hepburn, Yvonne John, Zoe Naus, Sue Newsome, Lucy Slimmon and to the three anonymous contributors. Thank you to UCLH neonatal unit for its incredible work.

For their encouragement/friendship/comments on some of these poems: Fiona Benson, Judy Brown, Isobel Dixon, Sasha Dugdale, Sarala Estruch, Alice Hiller, Bhanu Kapil, Kinara collective, Fiona Larkin, Michael Mackmin, Kathryn Maris, Ellen McAteer, Gita Ralleigh, Sally Read, Heidi Williamson. To Caroline, Afra and Kiara, Clare, Harpreet, HdS, Helen, Jay, Judith, Kate, Keith, Lisa, Louise, Sam, Will and others not mentioned here. A salute also to all the lost and found survivors.

Grateful thanks for various resources that helped me work on elements of this book 2018–2021: Arts Council England, the Society of Authors, Hosking Houses Trust and the Rebecca Swift Foundation.

Huge thanks to my editor Deryn Rees-Jones for her steadfast, warm and expert support especially during a hard pandemic year, and to Alison Welsby and the team at Pavilion Poetry, including

Lydia, Olivia and Alistair. Thank you especially to Dan, Alex and Ishy.

The term NOMO or NoMo was coined in 2011 by Jody Day as an abbreviation/contraction of 'not-mother'. Day is the founder of Gateway Women, an international support group for childless/childfree women.

Bloodfruit: An open call was put out just before the UK went into lockdown in March 2020 for people to share their difficult journeys towards mother/non-motherhood. Interviews were conducted via video-conferencing, and, with permission, transcribed and written up. Some fragments of text are verbatim, others mixed with the poet's own words. *Further resources*: fertilitynetworkuk.org; bliss.org.uk; tommys.org; gateway-women.com; mind.org.uk

Olive Ridley, from the eponymous poem, is an endangered species of sea turtle that nests on the coast of Odisha in India. 'The Good Doctor' was shortlisted for the Bridport Prize, 2020. 'Dodo Provocateur' used research from Errol Fuller's *Extinct Birds*. 'The Girl Who Would Be King' was written in response to Rudyard Kipling's story *The Man Who Would Be King*. 'Paperdolls *or* Where Are My Curly Scrolls of Sisters?' was commissioned by Kathryn Maris for *Poetry London* in response to artwork at A.P.T. Gallery. 'Manju' was longlisted for the National Poetry Competition 2019 and won third prize in the Poetry London Clore competition 2019. 'Routed' was commissioned and recorded for 'Dial-a-Poem', part of the Crossed Lines project supported by the AHRC and Nottingham Trent University (2020); www.crossedlines.co.uk

The old UK idiom 'on a hiding to nothing' reportedly derives from horse-racing/gambling odds and is commonly taken to mean that something or someone is going nowhere.

I actually like and use Cath Kidston's home accessories.